FALL 1997 SUPPLEMENT

DYNAMICS OF TRIAL PRACTICE: PROBLEMS AND MATERIALS

SECOND EDITION

By

Ronald L. Carlson
Fuller Callaway Professor of Law
University of Georgia

and

Edward J. Imwinkelried
Professor of Law
University of California at Davis

AMERICAN CASEBOOK SERIES

West Publishing Co.
St. Paul, Minn. 1997

ISBN 0–314–22744–X

TEXT IS PRINTED ON 10% POST
CONSUMER RECYCLED PAPER

PREFACE

In part, the purpose of this supplement is to update the primary text. For example, Chapter 3 of the supplement expands upon the list of factors that the attorney should consider in selecting a trial theory. Chapter 9 illustrates techniques for phrasing questions to ensure that the witness's testimony incorporates sensory imagery. Likewise, Chapter 10 lists additional techniques for dealing with non-responsive witnesses. Some of these updates reflect recent contributions to the trial advocacy literature. Other updates are based on comments by trial attorneys at a series of continuing legal education programs we have co-taught throughout the country for the National Practice Institute.

However, our main motivation in issuing this supplement is to provide the student with a much lengthier model voir dire examination for Chapter 4. In our experience, voir dire questioning is the most difficult part of the trial process for students to master. In retrospect, we have decided that the sample voir dire examination currently set out in { 4.11 is too short and superficial. This supplement includes a much longer model. The model includes the administration of the oath to the panel, judicial interrogation, questioning by the attorneys, strikes, and the administration of the final oath to the jury. We have had the model reviewed by several experienced trial judges to ensure that the sample is both realistic and complete. We hope that the new model will assist in the difficult task of teaching jury selection.

In closing, we would like to thank Judge Donna Petre of the California Superior Court and Mr. Jon Sands, adjunct professor at the Arizona State University College of Law. Judge Petre reviewed our new voir dire and circulated the draft among her colleagues. Mr. Sands, a longtime user of the text, has contributed numerous, excellent suggestions for improving this text.

Ronald L. Carlson
Edward J. Imwinkelried

TABLE OF CONTENTS

§ 3.3(D) Final Pretrial Case Evaluation

Page 34. Add after second full sentence on page:
In a recent case, Maxwell Blecher won a $72 million verdict for the plaintiffs in a lawsuit against Eastman Kodak. *Organize Complex Cases Clearly*, NAT'L L.J., May 13, 1996, at D3. Another attorney had drafted a "shotgun" complaint for the plaintiffs. However, at trial, Mr. Blecher decided to "abandon[] all but the monopoly claim." He explained: "The more claims you pile on, the more you can confuse. You go in with a rifle, not a shotgun. My style is to give the jury the simplest possible case."

Page 35. Add at the end of the paragraph devoted to factor (3):
Do not be content with a legalistic approach. Rench, *"We win by being persuaders--not the legal technicians the law schools taught us to be,"* 15 THE CHAMPION 51, 52 (July 1991). You need a theory "that satisfies both the head and the heart." McElhaney, *Briefs That Sing: A Winning Argument Is More Than a Stack of Legal Issues*, 83 A.B.A.J. 80 (Mar. 1997).

Page 36. Add at the end of the paragraph devoted to factor (6):
As a practical matter, you cannot rely on a theory requiring a finding of deliberate misconduct unless you have strong evidence of the person's motive to engage in such conduct. McElhaney, *Finding the Right Script*, 81 A.B.A.J. 90 (Aug. 1995).

Page 37. Add a new paragraph after the paragraph devoted to factor (8):
(9) Does the theory require the jurors to assume an extraordinary coincidence or an implausible occurrence? In the privacy of the deliberation room, the jurors' natural inclination is to rely on their everyday experience to help them choose between the competing versions of the facts urged by the parties. Moreover, in most jurisdictions, the judge will instruct them that they may draw on that experience in evaluating the testimony in the case. Suppose that you represent the defendant in a personal injury action resulting from a collision. Before trial, an accident reconstruction expert tells you that a third party driver merging from a freeway onramp could have caused the accident by driving either too slow or too fast. Other testimony indicates that the third party driver was probably a teenager. Relying on

stereotypes, the lay jurors are more likely to accept the hypothesis that the teenage driver was speeding.

§ 3.4. THE USE OF THE THEORY AND THEME AT TRIAL

§ 3.4(a) The Function of the Theory and Theme

Page 40. Add at the end of the carryover paragraph on the top of the page:

In the *Simpson* case, the prosecution deluged the jury with 99 days of testimony. *O.J. Trivia*, NAT'L L.J., Oct. 16, 1995. In the earlier *McMartin* child abuse trial, the prosecution called 124 witnesses and introduced 974 exhibits--requiring over 33 months of trial and consuming nearly 64,000 pages of transcript. Benedictis, *McMartin Preschool's Lessons: Abuse Case Plagued by Botched Investigation, Too Many Counts*, 76 A.B.A.J. 28 (Apr. 1990).

Add at the end of the next paragraph:

If the theme effectively encapsulates your best argument, the theme will help the jurors "to recall and restate" that argument "during deliberations." Crawford, *Make the Listening Easy for Jurors*, 32 TRIAL 54, 56 (June 1996).

§ 4.3 AN OVERVIEW OF JURY SELECTION PROCEDURES

Page 47. Add after first complete paragraph on page:

Formerly, it was merely helpful to use a diagram such as Figure 4-1. Hours or days might elapse between your questioning of a particular panelist and the judge's call for peremptory challenges; during that time lapse, you might forget the answer or gesture which makes it advisable to strike a particular panelist. However, modernly, the use of such diagrams is a virtual necessity. In the *Batson* lines of authority, the Supreme Court has announced that it is unconstitutional for any litigant--prosecutor, criminal defense attorney, or civil party--to exercise peremptory strikes on racist or sexist grounds. *Batson v. Kentucky*, 476 U.S. 79 (1986); *Edmonson v. Leesville Concrete Co.*, 500 U.S. 614 (1991); *Georgia v. McCollum*, 505 U.S. 42 (1992); *J.E.B. v. Alabama ex rel. T.B.*, 511 U.S. 127 (1994). If the opposing attorney accuses you of striking panelists on such unconstitutional grounds, you need to articulate a legitimate reason for removing the panelist. *Puckett v. Elem*, 115 S.Ct. 1769 (1995). To substantiate that reason, you may need to insert your marked diagram into the record. *E.g.*, *McCrory v. Henderson*, 871 F.Supp. 597 (W.D.N.Y. 1995); *Echlin v. Lecureux*, 800 F.Supp. 515 (E.D.Mich. 1992). The diagram will document your legitimate basis for exercising a strike against the panelist. The stakes are high. In some jurisdictions, on appeal a single *Batson* error is per se reversible error. *United States v. Annigoni*, 96 F.3d 1132 (9th Cir. 1996); *State v. Huerta*, 175 Ariz. 262, 855 P.2d 776 (1993).

§ 4.5 THE PERSPECTIVE OF THE QUESTIONING ATTORNEY--THE STRATEGY OF JURY DESELECTION

Page 49. Add at the end of the first paragraph in this section:

You do not want an "audience" which is positively hostile to your case. Bennett & Hirschhorn, *Conducting Meaning, Effective Voir Dire in Criminal Cases*, 17 THE CHAMPION 18, 19 (June 1993).

§ 4.6 THE PERSPECTIVE OF THE QUESTIONING ATTORNEY--PRETRIAL QUESTIONNAIRES

Page 52. Add after second paragraph in section:

Tailored questionnaries such as those employed in *Simpson* and *King* cases are now in widespread use. Fargo, *Juror Questionnaires Can Supplement Voir Dire*, 29 TRIAL 23 (Oct. 1993); James, *Voir Dire in the '90s*, THE PRACTICAL

LITIGATOR, Jan. 1995, at 29 (including a sample questionnaire). The American Bar Association has revised its STANDARDS FOR CRIMINAL JUSTCE: TRIAL BY JURY to regulate the content of questionnaires. 53 Crim.L. 2347 (Sep. 29, 1993). Standard 15-2.2 now provides:

> (a) Basic questionnaire
>
> Before voir dire examination begins, the court and counsel shall be provided with data pertinent to the qualifications of the prospective jurors and to matters ordinarily raised in voir dire examination.
>
> (1) The questionnaire should include information about the juror's name, sex, age, residence, marital status, education level, occupation, and occupation history, employment address, previous service as a juror, and present or past involvement as a party to civil or criminal litigation.
>
> (2) Such data should be obtained from prospective jurors by means of a questionnaire furnished to prospective jurors with the jury summons, and to be returned by the prospective jurors before the time of jury selection.
>
> (b) Specialized questionnaire
>
> In appropriate cases, the court, with the assistance of counsel, should prepare a specialized questionnaire addressing particular issues that may arise.
>
> (1) The questionnaire should be specific enough to provide appropriate information for utilization by counsel, but not be unnecessarily embarrassing or overly intrusive.
>
> (2) If questionnaires are made available to counsel prior to the day of voir dire, the identity of jurors may be protected by removing identifying information from the questionnaires.
>
> (c) All questionnaires should be prepared and supervised by the court.
>
> (1) The jurors should be advised of the purpose of the questionnaire, how it will be used and who will have access to the information.
>
> (2) All questionnaires should be provided to counsel in sufficient time before the start of voir dire to enable counsel to adequately review them before the start of voir dire.

§ 4.8 THE PERSPECTIVE OF THE QUESTIONING ATTORNEY--PLANNING AND CONDUCTING THE QUESTIONING AT TRIAL

§ 4.8(A) Listing All the Types of Questions That the Attorney Would Like to Ask

<u>Page 61. Add at the end of the first paragraph:</u>

Ahlen, *Voir Dire: What Can I Ask and What Can I Say?*, 72 N.D.L.REV. 631, 641 (1996). In a recent survey of successful litigators, all the litigators commenting on their voir dire strategy voiced the traditional view. One attorney, Paul Luvera, described the voir dire as "a race for the disclosure of" the damaging aspects of each party's case. *Point Out Flaws Early, Before They Harm Case*, NAT'L L.J., Feb. 14, 1994. Another litigator, Willie E. Gary, stated that during voir dire, he "admits any problems with his case. 'You have to steal their thunder.'" *He Works Hard to Win Cases Before They Are Filed*, NAT'L L.J., Feb. 14, 1994, at S8.

§ 4.11 SAMPLE VOIR DIRE EXAMINATION

Page 75. Add a new sample voir dire at the end of the section:

(To the entire jury panel after it has been sworn and seated) Ladies and gentlemen, I am now going to question all of you prospective jurors who are seated in the jury box concerning your qualifications to serve as jurors in this case. However, all members of this jury panel, whether in the jury box or those of you seated elsewhere in the courtroom, should pay close attention to my questions. You ought to make note of the answers you would give if these questions were put to you personally. If and when any other member of this panel is called to the jury box, he or she will be asked to give their answers to these questions.

In the trial of this case the parties are entitled to have a fair and unbiased jury. If there is any reason why any of you might be biased or prejudiced in any way, you must disclose that reason when you are asked to do so. It is your legal duty to make this disclosure.

This trial will likely take four days to complete, but it may take longer. Do any of you have any responsibilities at home or at work that would make it difficult or impossible to give us your full attention for this period of time? If you would, please raise your hand at this time.

(No hands are raised.)

The record will reflect that no panelist raised a hand.

Now let me give you some background about this case. This case is a personal injury action. The plaintiff, Mr. Peter Williams, is a desk clerk at the Senator Hotel in downtown Morena. The defendant, Mr. Robert Scott, was a guest staying at the hotel in January, 19YR-1. The plaintiff alleges that on January 19th of that year, the defendant and another man by the name of Richard Rogers attacked and beat him. The plaintiff also alleges that he suffered certain injuries in the attack. I want to emphasize that the plaintiffs' allegations are not evidence. The plaintiff will not only have to allege those things; he will have the burden of proving those things at this trial.

At this point, we need to find out whether you can serve as a fair juror in this case. We're not trying to pry, but we need to know whether you can be an impartial juror for this trial. For that reason, I'm going to ask you some questions; and then the attorneys will have a chance to question you. Before we do that, though, we need to put you under oath. Madame Bailiff, would you please administer the oath to the panel?

Yes, Your Honor. Ladies and gentlemen, all members of the panel, please stand. "Do you and each of you understand and agree that you will accurately and truthfully answer, under penalty of perjury, all questions propounded to you concerning your qualifications and competency to serve as a trial juror in a matter pending before this court and that failure to do so may subject you to criminal prosecution?" If so, say, "I do."

(All panelists respond, "I do.")

You may be seated.

The parties to this case and their respective attorneys are: Mr. Kenneth Clark representing the plaintiff Mr. Williams and Ms. Jill Peterson representing the defendant Mr. Scott. I'd like all the parties and their attorneys to stand. (to the jury panel) Ladies and gentlemen, have you heard of or been acquainted with any of these parties or their attorneys? Again, if you do, please raise your hand.

Do any of these people even look familiar to you? If so, just raise your hand.

During the trial of this case, the following witnesses may be called to testify on behalf of the parties. These witnesses are: Dr. Fred Amerson, Professor Anna Dulay, Police Officer Janice Taylor, Dr. Gina Jackson, Ms. Joan Freeman, and Mr. William K. S. Wang. Have any of you heard of or been otherwise acquainted with any of the witnesses just named?

Do any of those names even sound familiar to you?

Have any of you heard of, or have you any knowledge of, the facts or events in this case?

Do any of you have any belief or feeling toward any of the parties, attorneys, or witnesses that might be regarded as a prejudice for or against any of them?

Do you have any interest, financial or otherwise, in the outcome of this case?

Have any of you served as a juror or witness involving any of these parties, attorneys or witnesses?

Have any of you served as a juror in any case?

(A juror raises her hand.)

What is your name?

Ms. Palumbo, Your Honor.

Was it a civil or criminal case?

It was a criminal case, Your Honor.

You must understand that there is a basic difference between a civil case and a criminal case. In a criminal case a defendant must be found guilty beyond a reasonable doubt; in a civil case such as this, you need find only that the evidence you accept as the basis of your decision is more convincing, and thus has the greater probability of truth than the contrary evidence. The standard in this trial is lower than in a criminal case. The standard here is just a preponderance of the evidence.

Do you understand the difference between the two types of cases?

Yes, Your Honor.

And you realize that the plaintiff in this case doesn't have the same burden of proof as the prosecution in the earlier criminal case you sat on. Correct?

Yes.

Very well. Let's shift to another topic then. Have any of you, or any member of your family or close friends to your knowledge, ever sued anyone, or has there ever been a claim presented against any of you, or to your knowledge against any member of your family or close friends, in connection with a matter similar to this case?

Are any of you, or any member of your family or close friends to your knowledge, presently involved in a lawsuit of any kind?

Have any of you, or any member of your family or close friends, had any special training in investigating criminal offenses?

In this case, you may be called upon to award damages for the plaintiff's claimed personal injury, including pain and suffering. Do any of you have any religious or other belief that pain and suffering are not real or any belief that would prevent you from awarding damages for pain and suffering if the defendant's liability for them is established?

Are there any of you who would not employ a medical doctor?

To your knowledge, have you or any member of your family ever been in an incident with the result that a claim for personal injuries or for substantial property damage was made by someone involved in that incident, whether or not a lawsuit was filed?

Have you or they, to your knowledge, ever been involved in a situation in which someone died or received serious personal injuries, whether or not a lawsuit was filed?

In this case, Mr. Williams claims that he has suffered permanent injuries to his arms, legs, and back. Do any of you, or any member of your family or close friends to your knowledge, currently suffer from similar injuries? Have you or they, to your knowledge, suffered from similar injuries in the past?

It is important that I have your assurance that you will, without reservation, follow my instructions on the law and will apply that law to this case. To put it somewhat differently, whether you approve or disapprove of the courts' instructions, it is your solemn duty to accept them as correct these statements of the law. You may not substitute your own idea of what you think the law ought to be. Will all of you follow the law as given to you by me in this case?

I am now going to allow the attorneys to ask you some questions. Before they do that, though, would each of you should now state the information listed on the chalkboard over there. As you can see, it asks you to state your name, where you live, your marital status--whether married, single, widowed or divorced--the number and ages of your children if any, your occupational history, and the name of your present employer. If you are married, you should also describe briefly your spouse's occupational history and present employer, if any. Please begin with juror number one.

My name is Margaret Marcetti. I reside at 347 San Benito Way in Morena. I work for State Farm Insurance Company. I'm divorced, and I have one child, a nine year old son.

Now juror number two.

Yes, Your Honor. My name is Harvey Leader. I live at 1051 Felton St. here in Morena. I'm single with no dependents. I work at a Circuit City warehouse.

Juror number three.

My name is Reverend Wiley Morris. I live and work at the New Life Evangelistic Center on the 2200 block of Mission Street here in town. I'm married and have two children. My wife is also a counselor at the center.

Juror number four.

My name is Elaine Palumbo. I'm a graduate student in psychology at the University of El Dorado. I live in an apartment near campus. I'm engaged to be married to Brandon Lowenthal. He's a physician at Morena Med School.

Juror number five.

My name is Jan Gilligan. I'm retired military--I spent 30 years on active duty with the Marine Corps. I'm a widower. I live in Condo Unit C, 239 Castro Street. I have two kids. They're both grown. One lives in Hong Kong, and the other is in Palo Alto, California.

Now juror number six.

Right, Your Honor. My name is Jesus Castro. I live at 3344 18th Avenue in Morena. I have my own business, a small specialized computer programming firm. I've been married for ten years. My wife Elizabeth and I have two kids, Tomas and Teresa.

Ladies and gentlemen, please think carefully. Do any of you know of any factor, whether or not I have asked about it, that might influence your view of this case? Has anything occurred during this questioning period that might make you doubt whether you would be a completely fair and impartial juror in this case? If there is, it is your legal duty to disclose the reason at this time.

All right. Mr. Clark, you may question the panel.

(Plaintiff's Questions)

Thank you, Your Honor. Ladies and gentlemen, my name is Kenneth Clark. I represent the plaintiff in this case, Mr. Peter Williams. Mr. Williams contends that on January 19, 19YR-1, the defendant and a Dick Rogers punched and kicked him at the Senator Hotel. The defendant denies that he was involved in the attack. That's why you're here today--to decide that dispute. As her Honor indicated, I'm going to ask you a few questions now. At the very beginning, I want to make it clear that Ms. Peterson and I need to ask you these questions just to ensure that you can be fair to both Mr. Williams and the defendant. I want to apologize in advance if any of my questions seem to pry into your privacy. I want to assure you that we're questioning you just to make certain that you can be an impartial juror to decide this dispute.

Ms. Marcetti, let's start with you. I'd like to ask you a few questions now.

You said that you work for State Farm Insurance Company. How long have you worked for them?

About nine years now.

Specifically, what is your job?

I handle earthquake and flood insurance for this area.

Do you handle personal liability claims like claims for injuries resulting from incidents such as fights?

No.

Have you ever handled personal liability claims?

No.

Does anyone in your office handle that type of claim?

No. There are a couple of State Farm offices in Morena. We're out in the Avenues. There's another office downtown, and that's where they take care of all the auto stuff.

Having worked for an insurance company for so long, do you think that you'd tend to side with the defense in this case?

No. Not necessarily.

You said "not necessarily." In your mind, what would it depend on?

The facts. Some good claims come across my desk, and I see some bad ones too. I try to be fair. If the facts show that it's a bad claim, I turn it down. But if the facts show that it's a good claim, I pay it. I have insurance too, and I resent it when I'm in the right and my insurer drags it feet paying the claim. Like I said, it all depends on the facts.

Let's talk for a moment about some of the facts in this case. Ms. Marcetti, in this case there's going to be evidence that about half an hour before the attack, Mr. Williams had been drinking. To be specific, he had three boilermakers--a shot and a beer. What do you think about people who drink?

It's O.K.. I drink sometimes. It all depends on how much you drink and the social setting. As I said, it depends.

Do you have any religious objections to drinking?

No.

Do you belong to any organizations that oppose drinking? You know--organizations like MADD, Mothers Against Drunk Driving.

No.

Have you ever belonged to such an organization?

Never.

Do you think that Mr. Williams' identification of his attackers is automatically wrong just because he had those three drinks?

Of course not.

Would you consider all the evidence before deciding whether Mr. Williams' identification is reliable?

Yes.

For example, would you listen carefully to the evidence about how well Mr. Williams tolerates liquor--how well he "holds" his liquor?

Yes.

Can you promise Mr. Williams that you won't reject his testimony simply because he had been drinking?

Yes.

At the end of this case, Judge Smith will give you an instruction about the law in the State of El Dorado on eyewitness identification. It's an instruction that tells you how to decide whether to believe an identification such as Mr. Williams' identification of the identification. Her Honor is going to tell you that you're supposed to consider how close Mr. Williams was to his attackers? Will you do your best to follow her Honor's instruction?

Yes.

Will you carefully consider the testimony about how close Mr. Williams was to the two men who attacked him?

Yes.

Her Honor may also instruct you that you're supposed to consider how long Mr. Williams had to view his attackers. If her Honor gives you that instruction, will you do your level best to follow it?

Yes.

Can you promise us that you'll pay close attention to the evidence of how long Mr. Williams had to observe his attackers?

I'll certainly try.

We appreciate that. Thank you very much, Ms. Marcetti.

Mr. Leader, I'd like to speak with you next. A few moments ago you heard Judge Smith describe the accident involving the plaintiff and Mr. Wade. I notice from your juror questionnaire that you live near the Senator Hotel. Are you familiar with the hotel?

Sure. It's one of the oldest hotels in downtown, and that's pretty near where I work.

Did you happen to witness any attack at the hotel in January of 19YR-1?

No.

As far as you know, did any of your friends and neighbors happen to witness this incident?

No, not as far as I know.

Have you read anything in the newspapers about the facts of this case?

If I did, I sure don't remember doing that.

Have you heard any reports on the radio or television about the facts of this case?

Nope.

O.K. Mr. Leader, could you please tell us something about your line of work.

I work as a warehouseman.

How long have you worked as a warehouseman?

About 10 years.

Exactly what are your duties as a warehouseman?

Well, let's put it this way. I'm not the white collar guy who sits in the office and shuffles paper. I'm the blue collar guy who actually pushes the boxes around in the warehouse. I do the manual labor.

While you've worked as a warehouseman, did you know of any co-workers who suffered from back pain?

Sure.

Did they ever put in a day's work even though they had that type of pain?

Of course.

Have you yourself ever had a day when you had sharp back pain?

If it was really sharp, I'd get the day off; but in that job, it's pretty common to have some back pain.

Did you work despite the pain?

Sure. I need the paycheck.

Given your experience, what do you think about awarding money damages to plaintiffs for pain and suffering? Mr. Williams is asking for money damages for pain and suffering. Do you think that's fair?

I'm not sure I understand the question.

I'm sorry. Let me put it this way. Some people don't think courts have any business awarding money for something like pain. Other people believe that you should treat pain like any other injury caused by an accident--you should give money damages for pain in the same way you give them for lost wages. As between those two views, who would you tend to agree with?

I guess I'd have to agree with the second group of people. It's one thing if you have to put up with the pain because it's your line of work. That's part of what you get paid for. But it's different if someone is at fault and causes you to suffer the pain. In a way, I can see how you should be paid for that.

Thank for, Mr. Leader. Suppose that at the end of this trial, Judge Smith instructs you that if you find Mr. Scott liable, you must award Mr. Williams money damages for pain and suffering. Can you promise me that you'd follow that instruction?

Yes, sir.

And will you listen carefully to the testimony you'll hear during the trial about the extent of Mr. Williams' pain and suffering?

Yeah.

Mr. Leader, let's talk a bit more about Mr. Williams' injuries. In this case, to prove his injuries, Mr. Williams is going to call a number of doctors, medical experts. They're going to testify about "soft tissue" injuries--injuries you're not going to be able to see on any chart or X-ray.

Think back. Have you ever accidentally banged your arm or leg against a door? You hit it real hard, but you didn't cut yourself. That ever happen to you?

I guess so.

In that situation, you couldn't see any blood. Could you?

No. Not unless it was a real bad one.

And you didn't necessarily develop a black-and-blue bruise. Did you?

No.

But was the pain real? Did you really feel the pain even though you couldn't see any blood or bruise?

Sure.

You've had that personal experience. Would you then reject the expert's testimony about "soft tissue" injuries simply because the doctors won't be able to produce any X-rays to show you the injuries?

I don't think so. I'd try to listen to what the doc had to say.

At the end of the trial, Judge Smith will give you some instructions about the damages which Mr. Williams suffered. If Judge Smith instructs you that you should award Mr. Williams money damages for "soft tissue" injuries, can you assure Mr. Williams that you'll try to carry out Judge Smith's instruction?

Yes, I would. I'd do my best to do what the judge says.

And can you promise Mr. Williams that you'll listen carefully to what his doctors have to say about those injuries?

I'll try.

Thank you. Reverend Morris, I'd like to chat with you now. I have just a couple of questions. Now as I recall, a few minutes ago you said that you are affiliated with the New Life Evangelistic Center. Is that correct?

Yes.

I have to confess that I'm unfamiliar with that center. Could you tell us a little about it?

I'd be glad to. We are a Christian church organization. We have a shelter for the homeless, and on a daily basis we provide free meals for the poor. We also provide counseling services. I work primarily in the counseling function.

And you're a minister in this organization?

Yes. I am.

Now I know that some Christian organizations have scruples against using physicians. They believe in faith healing. My client, Mr. Williams, used a physician after this incident, and he's going to be asking the jury in this case to compensate for thousands of dollars in medical expenses. Do you personally believe in faith healing?

As a Christian, I do believe in miracles. I think that sometimes prayer can bring about miraculous medical recoveries.

Have you ever personally been acquainted with someone who you thought experienced a miraculous cure?

No. I can't say that I have.

Do you have any religious problems with people consulting physicians about medical problems?

None at all.

You said that you counsel people who come to the center. Do you ever counsel people with medical problems?

Of course.

Have you ever recommended that any of them seek professional medical help for those problems?

On many occasions. I do some work with people who have substance abuse problems. I strongly recommend that they go to see physicians, psychiatrists, and psychologists. I believe in that.

I take it then that you wouldn't have any problems awarding money damages for medical expenses?

No, at least not if I thought that the defendant was liable and the medical expenses were reasonable.

One last topic, Reverend Morris. A couple of minutes ago I was speaking with Ms. Marcetti. We were talking about the fact that Mr. Williams had had some drinks. She told us that she had no religious scruples against drinking. Do you?

No. I'm like her. It all depends on whether a person drinks in moderation. If they go too far, I do think it's sinful.

Do you personally use alcohol?

Rarely but sometimes.

Do you ever have parties at the center?

Yes.

Do you ever serve beer or liquor at the parties?

Sometimes we serve beer.

Can you promise Mr. Williams that you'll listen carefully to his testimony and not reject it just because he had those drinks?

I can assure you that in good conscience.

Thank you very much, Reverend. Ms. Palumbo, can I ask you a few questions now?

Certainly.

Ms. Palumbo, when her Honor was questioning you, you said that you're engaged to a physician at Morena Med School. Does my memory serve me well?

Yes, it does. My fiance is Dr. Lowenthal.

What is Dr. Lowenthal's specialty?

He's a brain surgeon.

I assume that he had training in general surgery before he developed his specialty.

That's a safe assumption. I vaguely recall a rotation in general surgery.

In this case, my client, Mr. Williams, will be calling several orthopedic surgeons to testify about the extent of his injuries. To your knowledge, has your fiance ever done that type of surgery?

I would suppose so.

To the best of your memory, has he ever discussed that type of surgery with you?

He might have, but I honestly can't recall.

So he's never made any statements to you that might influence your evaluation of the testimony by Mr. Williams' witnesses?

None that I can remember.

And do you understand that if you serve on the jury in this case and you have any questions about the testimony about those witnesses, you won't be permitted to put those questions to your fiance?

Certainly.

Can you promise Mr. Williams that you'll base your evaluation of that testimony solely on the evidence you would hear in this courtroom?

Yes. I can give you that assurance.

There's one other topic I'd like to take up with you. Mr. Williams is 65 years old. Do you live with any elderly people?

I'm not sure that I understand the question.

I'm sorry. Let me put it this way. Have you ever lived in the same house with someone who was 60 years of age or older?

No. I guess not. When I left home, my parents were both in their 40's.

Do you think that elderly people necessarily have grudges against young people?

No. It depends on the person. I'd hate to generalize about something like that. I don't think stereotypes are very useful.

Do you think that elderly persons necessarily have difficulty making identifications?

Well, your vision sometimes deteriorates when you get older, but it doesn't necessarily happen. You've got to know the facts about the eyesight of the individual in question. Again, it largely depends on the person.

So you wouldn't reject Mr. Williams' identification simply because he was 65 at the time of this incident?

No. I certainly wouldn't do that.

Thank you Ms. Palumbo. Mr. Williams appreciates that. Now Mr. Gilligan, I have some questions for you.

O.K.

Mr. Gilligan, as I recall, you said that you are a retired member of the Marine Corps.

Yup.

What was your military specialty?

I was an artillery officer.

Did you ever serve as a juror in a court-martial?

On several occasions.

Those were criminal trials. Correct?

Yes.

Do you understand that although the standard of proof is beyond a reasonable doubt in a criminal trial, the standard is only a preponderance of the evidence in a civil case like this one?

I realize that. The judge talked about that before.

And you won't hold Mr. Williams to the higher burden, proof beyond a reasonable doubt, in deciding whether she had proven her case?

Of course not.

Mr. Gilligan, when you were on active duty in the military, were women permitted to serve in combat roles?

Not at that time. That's changed since I left active duty.

Do you agree with that change?

To be frank, I was a little skeptical at first. However, the change has been in effect for a while now, and the feedback I've gotten from my friends still on active duty is that it's worked out real well.

In this case, Mr. Williams is going to calling Police Officer Janice Taylor as a witness. She's a female member of the Morena Police Department. What you think about women in the police force?

I've got no problem with that. They might be as good at stopping a violent crime, but that's only part of their job.

Let's talk about a specific part of a police officer's job, namely, investigating a crime. Officer Taylor is going to testify about her investigation of the attack on Mr. Williams. Do you have any doubts that a female police officer would be competent to handle that job?

No. I knew several female MPs--military police. They were highly competent. In one case in particular I was involved in, it was a female MP whose investigation cracked it. Her work in that case was just plain outstanding.

Mr. Gilligan, that's good to hear. Now have you listened carefully to the questions I've asked the other jurors--the questions, for example, about awarding money damages for personal injuries?

I tried to be attentive as best I could.

Would you have answered any of those questions differently than they did?

I don't believe so.

Thank you. Finally, Mr. Castro, I need to speak with for a while. You told us that you own your own business. Have you ever been sued?

No.

Have you ever had to sue one of your customers?

Thankfully no.

So do you have any general impressions of attorney who represent plaintiffs or attorneys who represent defendants at civil trials?

No. I haven't had any personal dealings in lawsuits. You read things in the papers, but I haven't had any direct contact with trial attorneys other than Ms. Marcus who does my legal work.

You said that you "read things in the papers." What things have you read?

Well, to be honest, there a lot of negative things in the papers about attorneys. Everyone knows that.

Like what?

You sometimes read that plaintiffs' attorneys bring unfounded lawsuits against businesses.

Do you think that those statements are true?

Sometimes, but you can't take what you read it the papers at face value. I've certainly learned that over the years. When you read the silly articles about computer technology in the papers, you realize how off base they are on the facts a lot of the time.

In this case Mr. Williams is the plaintiff. You don't necessarily think that he's in the wrong simply because he's the plaintiff who brought this suit and he's asking for money damages?

No, of course not. You have to consider the specific facts of the case before you make up your mind.

Fine, Mr. Castro. No other questions, Your Honor.

Court: Ms. Peterson, you may question now.

(Defense Questions)

Thank you, Your Honor.

Ms. Marcetti, my name is Jill Peterson. I represent the defendant in this case, Mr. Robert Scott. As plaintiff's counsel indicated, Mr. Scott denies that he was at fault in injuring the plaintiff. Mr. Scott freely admits that he was at the hotel the night of the attack, but he maintains that he had nothing to do with the attack on the plaintiff. I want to ask you a couple of questions to see whether you'd be comfortable sitting as a juror in this dispute between Mr. Scott and the plaintiff.

A few minutes ago the plaintiff's attorney indicated that one of the witnesses in this case is likely to be Officer Janice Taylor. She's a member of the Morena Police Department. Have you ever worked for a police department?

No.

Do you have any relatives who work for a police department?

No.

Do you have any friends who work for a police department?

I've got a neighbor down the street who I think works for the police, but I'm not even sure about that.

Let's suppose that Officer Taylor testifies in this case. Do you think that police officers are generally more truthful than other people?

No. They're just human beings. There are good ones and bad ones.

Do you think that the testimony of police officers is entitled to more weight than the testimony of other citizens?

No. It all depends on the facts. I get statements from policemen in the files I process. Some of the statements are great, and some of them are just plain garbage. It depends on the person.

Later in this case Her Honor may instruct you that you are to judge Officer Taylor's testimony the same way you judge the testimony of all the other witnesses in the case. If she gives you that instruction, will you be able to follow it?

Sure.

And you won't give Officer Taylor's testimony any special consideration just because she works for the police?

No.

Let's take another step. Officer Taylor might end up giving some expert opinions in this case--conclusions that a normal layperson couldn't give on the witness stand. Do you think you should accept a person's opinion just because they're an expert?

Not at all.

In your work, do you often receive statements from people who call themselves experts?

All the time.

How do you go about deciding whether to rely on those statements?

I look at their qualifications. I see if they have any biases, and I try to figure out whether their conclusion makes sense in terms of the facts. Over the years in my job I've learned to trust the facts more than particular witnesses.

Her Honor may instruct that you are not to accept expert opinions at face value simply because the witness is an expert. Could you follow that instruction?

I'll have no difficulty with that one. I can guarantee you that.

Mr. Leader, let me ask you some questions now. As her Honor said a few minutes ago, there may be a large number of witnesses in this case. However, at this point we intend to call only two witnesses, Mr. Scott and a Ms. Joan Freeman.

Have you ever been in a situation where some of your friends were having a disagreement--a couple of friends said one thing <u>but</u> one friend said something else?

Oh, I suppose so.

When you were in that situation, did you think that the last friend was necessarily wrong just because he or she was outnumbered, just because there were more people on the other side of the argument?

No. Not necessarily. It depends on who's on which side and what they have to say. You use your common sense.

O.K. So you'd listen to what your friend had to say even if there were more people on the other side.

Sure.

Now, later in this case, Judge Smith is going to give you an instruction. She's going to tell you that you shouldn't decide this case simply on the basis of the number of witnesses called by the two sides. You can't decide who's right just by counting the number of witnesses on the two sides. Can you promise me that if Judge Smith gives you that instruction, you'll try your level best to follow it?

Yes.

And you won't reject the defense's testimony simply because the plaintiff may call more witnesses?

No.

Thank you, Mr. Leader. Let's turn to you now, Reverend Morris. Reverend, I was talking to Ms. Marcetti about Officer Taylor. There's going to be some evidence in this case about a statement Mr. Scott made to the officer. The evidence is going to show that when she awoke him from his sleep and asked him about his shoes, he said that he might have lent the shoes to a friend. He'll testify in this trial that he said that only because he was a big sleepy and angry about being awakened. He'll admit that he didn't lend those shoes to anyone.

Would you reject his testimony in this case simply because he made that statement to Officer Taylor?

I'm not sure I understand.

I'm sorry. Let's suppose that a person says one thing before trial and then says something else on the witness stand. Does that necessarily mean that they're lying on the stand?

No. You'd have to know all the facts.

What facts would you want to know?

Well, I'd want to know why they made the statement before trial.

So can you promise Mr. Scott that you'll listen to his testimony explaining his statement to Officer Taylor?

Certainly. You can't leap to judgments about people. That's one thing I've learned in my work.

Thank you, Reverend Morris. Ms. Palumbo, I have just a couple of questions for you. You told us that you're graduate student in psychology at U.E.D.?

Yes.

What is the focus of your graduate research?

I'm reviewing the validity studies of intelligence tests. Specifically, I'm looking into the question of whether there really is racial bias in some or all of those tests.

Does your graduate course work include any research into the process of memory?

No.

I'd presume, though, that as an undergraduate psychology student, you spent some time studying the process of memory.

Sure. That's basic material in introductory psych courses.

Did you spend any time reviewing the studies of the reliability of eyewitness testimony?

A bit.

Did you form any strong opinions about the reliability of the memory of eyewitnesses to events?

Not really. Some psychologists believe that eyewitness memories are quite untrustworthy, but the research struck me as rather inconclusive. They need to investigate that further.

Now in this case, the plaintiff is going to be presenting his own testimony supposedly identifying Mr. Scott as one of the men who beat the plaintiff. At the end of the trial, her Honor is going to give you an instruction on eyewitness identification testimony. She's going to tell you that one of the factors you should consider is the state of mind of the person who made the identification?

Would your educational background made it difficult for you to follow that instruction?

I don't see why it would. Quite apart from the research, it's just common sense that the person's frame of mind would be relevant.

So you'd listen carefully to the evidence about Mr. Williams' state of mind--for example, what he was thinking about just before he was attacked on the second floor. Right?

Sure.

Very well, Ms. Palumbo.

Now, Mr. Gilligan, you said that you have two grown children. What lines of work are they in?

My daughter, Denise, is the export-import business. She works for a Hong Kong firm, and she lives there. My son, Chris, is an attorney.

Where does he work?

He lives and works in Silicon Valley in California.

What type of work does he do?

He does legal work for some of the computer firms there.

Does he do trials? Is he involved in litigation?

Not as far as I can tell. He does what he calls "transactional work." He puts together deals. He almost never goes to court as far as I can tell.

Has he ever expressed any preference for plaintiffs' attorneys or defense attorneys?

No. As I said, he never gets involved in trials. That's just not his bag. He likes to draft documents and negotiate deals. He doesn't touch the trial work.

Are there other attorneys in his firm who litigate--who go to trial?

No. My impression is that they refer the litigation to other firms. They don't become involved in trials. They farm that out.

One last topic. The evidence in this case is probably going to show that one of the men who attacked the plaintiff was a Dick Rogers. The evidence will also show that Mr. Scott knew Mr. Rogers. If the evidence shows that Rogers was at fault, would you automatically tend to think that Mr. Scott also had to be involved?

Just because they were friends?

Right.

No. I don't believe in guilt by association. If you're coming to find someone at fault, you've got to show that they were personally, individually responsible. I feel very strongly about that as a matter of principle.

Thank you very much, Mr. Gilligan. Mr. Castro, I'd like to speak with you now. What specifically does your business do?

We do specialized computer programmming.

Are any of your past or present clients law firms?

A few.

Were they firms that do trial work?

I think some of them were. We put together some innovative litigation support programs for them.

Let's talk about these firms for a second. Were they all plaintiffs' firms, firms that represented plaintiffs in lawsuits?

I honestly can't tell you. When I was doing the job, I had to find out the type of information they wanted to extract from the database; but that didn't require me to find whom they represented. It was a matter of indifference to me. It never occurred me to ask.

Now you've sat here and listened to Mr. Clark and I question the other five potential jurors. I asked a lot of questions--for example, whether you'd decide a case simply on the basis of the number of witnesses called by the two sides. Would you have answered any of the questions differently than the other panel members?

I don't believe so.

Is there anything in your personal background that might make it difficult for you to listen carefully to Mr. Scott's testimony in this case and evaluate it impartially?

Not that I can think of.

Thank you very much, Mr. Castro. No further questions, Your Honor.

Court: Attorneys, please approach. Are there any challenges for cause?

Attorneys: No.

Court: Very well. Please resume your seats.

(The attorneys return to their respective counsel tables.)

All right. Are there any challenges? Mr. Clark, you first.

Your Honor, we'd like you to thank and excuse Mr. Leader.

Mr. Leader, we're going to excuse you from service on this jury. I do want to thank you. I'd like you to return to the jury pool room. Juror number seven, Mr. Furnish, please take Mr. Leader's seat.

Mr. Furnish. Before I allow the attorneys to question you, I'd like you to give us the items of information listed on the chalkboard.

Yes, Your Honor. My name is Don Furnish. I live at 28 Huntington Drive in Morena out in the Avenues. I'm single. I'm not married, and I never have been. I'm a native Morenan. I teach History at Lowell High School here in the City.

Mr. Clark, you may question, but please keep it brief. We're running out of the time allotted for jury selection. This has run a little longer that I expected. We have only a couple of minutes left.

Yes, Your Honor. I'll be brief.

Mr. Furnish, I've noticed that you've been listening carefully while we talked to the other members of the panel. As you know, we've asked questions about such things as people's beliefs about drinking and awarding money damages for pain and suffering? Please think carefully. Would you have answered any of those questions differently?

No.

Your Honor, I have no further questions of Mr. Furnish.

Court: Ms. Peterson?

Your Honor, Mr. Scott would be perfectly happy with Mr. Furnish as a juror.

Very well. Ladies and gentlemen, we've been questioning you for well over an hour. I know that we've asked you a lot of questions, but it's always that we've overlooked something. I want you to think carefully. Is there any fact that we've neglected to ask about that would make it difficult for you to be a fair, impartial juror in this trial?

Very well. Mr. Clark, any further challenges?

No, Your Honor. Mr. Williams will be happy with this jury.

Ms. Peterson?

We pass for cause.

All right. Madame Bailiff, please swear the jury.

Yes, Your Honor. Please stand again. "Do you and each of you understand and agree that you will well and truly try the cause now pending before this court, and render a true verdict according only to the evidence presented to you and the instructions of the court?" If so, say, "I do."

(All the panelists respond, "I do.")

Ladies and gentlemen, we have our jury.

CHAPTER 5. OPENING STATEMENT--AN EXERCISE IN RES IPSA LOQUITUR

§ 5.5 THE STRUCTURE OF AN OPENING STATEMENT

§ 5.5(A) The Beginning

Page 82. Add after the first sentence in the second paragraph:

Before you rush to the historical merits of the case, "[p]ut[] a human face on [the] legal problem." Reidinger, *Spinning Yarns*, 82 A.B.A.J. 102 (June 1996).

§ 5.5(D) The Preview of the Evidence

Page 90. Add at the end of the first full paragraph on the page:

If a particular exhibit plays a central role in your case, invoke the judge's discretion and seek permission to display the exhibit during opening. *People v. Green*, 47 Cal.2d 209, 302 P.2d 307 (1956), allowed the playing of a motion picture during opening; and *People v. Kirk*, 43 Cal.App.3d 921, 117 Cal.Rptr. 345 (1974), permitted an attorney to play an audiotape during opening. Under Federal Rule of Evidence 103(a)(2), make a detailed offer of proof demonstrating that the exhibit will prove to be admissible during your case-in-chief.

CHAPTER 6. EVIDENTIARY OBJECTIONS--EFFECTIVELY URGING OBJECTIONS WHICH MAKE STRATEGIC OR TACTICAL SENSE

§ 6.2 RAISING EVIDENTIARY OBJECTIONS BEFORE TRIAL

Page 103. Add new paragraph before last paragraph on page:

If you raise the issue before trial, when you describe the evidentiary basis you can go into more detail than you can ordinarily do during trial. That advantage can be especially important if you are pressing an objection under Federal Rule of Evidence 403. Under that rule, the judge must weigh the probative value of the proffered evidence against any attendant probative dangers such as prejudice.

--If possible, minimize the probative value of the evidence by tendering a stipulation to the ultimate fact which the proponent is offering the item of evidence to prove. Suppose, for example, that the accused is charged with being a felon in possession of a firearm and that the prosecution attempts to introduce the record of the accused's prior conviction for a heinous offense to establish his or her status as a felon. The defense attorney might offer to stipulate that a conviction occurred, in order to bar introduction of the full record. That is precisely the tactic employed by a defense lawyer in a case which was resolved by the United States Supreme Court in early 1997. The prosecutor had rejected the offer to stipulate, and the trial judge refused to compel the prosecutor to accept it. This was error, said the Supreme Court. *Old Chief v. United States*, 117 S.Ct. 644 (1997). You will be in a better position to know what stipulations you can afford to tender if you have conducted a thorough, pretrial strategic evaluation of your case.

--In the memorandum supporting your *in limine* motion, cite empirical studies establishing the prejudicial nature of the evidence proffered by the proponent. The Chicago Jury Project researchers found that the typical juror regards certain misconduct such as official corruption as particularly despicable. H. KALVEN & H. ZEISEL, THE AMERICAN JURY 396-401 (1966). More recently, the Justice Department's Bureau of Justice Statistics conducted a National Survey of Crime Severity to determine how the public perceives the relative seriousness of various offenses. 60,000 citizens were surveyed. The survey found that homicides, rapes, and drug offenses were the highest rated crimes. The survey is detailed in the January 1984 issue of the Bureau of Justice Statistics Bulletin. Do not simply cry "wolf." Substantiate your claim of prejudice by pointing to research, ideally research conducted by the government itself.

§ 6.3 TYPICAL EVIDENTIARY OBJECTIONS AT TRIAL

§ 6.3(E) Object

The Phrasing of the Objection

Page 110. Add new paragraph after the carryover paragraph on top of page:

As the preceding paragraph suggests, when you are objecting to questions posed on direct examination, the basic theme of your objections should be that the proponent is attempting to introduce untrustworthy evidence. When you are challenging questions posed on cross-examination, the theme is often that the cross-examiner is treating the witness unfairly. Suppose, for example, that the cross-examiner inquires about an untruthful act under Federal Rule of Evidence 608(b) even without a good faith basis in fact for believing that the witness committed the act. C. MUELLER & L. KIRKPATRICK, MODERN EVIDENCE {{ 6.40-.41 (1995). The cross-examiner has an obligation to question in good faith. *Sanders-El v. Wencewicz*, 987 F.2d 483 (8th Cir. 1993)(while questioning a party about his prior criminal record, the cross-examiner "dramatically dropped in front of the jury . . . what look[ed] like about 10 feet of paper"). In this situation, you can not only object; with righteous indignation in your voice, in the hearing of the jury you can accuse the cross-examiner of "bad faith misconduct." *See* Carlson, *Objections at Trial: Putting New Wine in Old Wineskins*, 7 CR.L.ADV.RPTR. No. 5 (May 1997). Again in the jury's hearing, ask that the judge "admonish" the cross-examiner.

§ 7.2 DRAFTING A LINE OF QUESTIONS TO LAY A FOUNDATION FOR AN ITEM OF EVIDENCE

§ 7.2(H) Drafting the Foundational Questions

Page 132. Add at the end of the last full paragraph on the page:

You should not only incorporate sensory imagery in the phrasing of your questions; even more importantly, the phrasing should encourage the witness to use such imagery. Consider these illustrations: "Could you help the jury see what you saw when you came around the corner? Would you help us picture how cousin Charles was acting when Uncle Waldo signed his will? Ms. Williams, take us with you to that meeting. Could you show us how people reacted when the chairman announced that the company was going to start making assault rifles?" McElhaney, *Making Evidence*, 81 A.B.A.J. 84, 86 (Sep. 1995).

CHAPTER 8. THE MICROCOSM OF CROSS-EXAMINATION: IMPEACHMENT--MAKING FACTUAL ASSERTIONS UNDER THE GUISE OF ASKING QUESTIONS

§ 8.2 DRAFTING A LINE OF QUESTIONS TO LAY A FOUNDATION FOR AN ITEM OF IMPEACHMENT EVIDENCE

§ 8.2(E) Drafting the Foundational Questions

Page 157. Add at the end of the first full paragraph on the page:

Frankly, you want to "goad" the witness "into a fight." McElhaney, *Prepping the CEO*, 82 A.B.A.J. 84 (Oct. 1996). In closing argument, you will then be able to tell the jury that during cross, "they caught a glimpse of the real M. Clayton Ransom . . . ." *Id.*

CHAPTER 9. THE MACROCOSM OF DIRECT EXAMINATION: ORGANIZING THE CASE-IN-CHIEF--USING THE THEORY AND THEME TO BRACKET YOUR CASE

§ 9.2 STRUCTURING THE DIRECT EXAMINATION OF EACH WITNESS

§ 9.2(A) The Sequence of Topics on Direct

Page 176. Add after the first complete sentence on the page:
If you want the jurors to "connect" with your witnesses, show the jurors that witnesses are "real people." McElhaney, *The Human Factor*, 80 A.B.A.J. 84 (Nov. 1994).

§ 9.3 DETERMINING THE SEQUENCE OF THE WITNESSES

Page 180. On the top of the page substitute "The Hollow Men" for "The Love Song of J. Alfred Profrock."[1]

§ 9.4 PREPARING THE WITNESSES FOR TRIAL

Page 181. Add after the last full sentence on the page:
There are now CD-ROM products which serve the same purpose. One such product, "Be Prepared! for Your Deposition," not only reviews the mechanics and techniques of testifying; the product even includes tests which the user can take after reviewing each segment to ensure that he or she understands the mechanics and techniques. Bayer & Cohen, *Multimedia: Preparing Your Client for Deposition*, LEGAL TIMES, June 3, 1996, at 28.

---

[1] The authors wish to express their thanks to Mr. Jon Sands, Assistant Federal Public Defender for the District of Arizona and adjunct professor at Arizona State University College of Law, for calling this error to our attention.

CHAPTER 10. THE MACROCOSM OF CROSS-EXAMINATION--USING THE OPPOSING WITNESSES TO SUPPORT YOUR THEORY AND THEME

§ 10.2 PLANNING AND CONDUCTING A CROSS-EXAMINATION OR RECROSS

§ 10.2(E) Choosing the Purposes to Pursue During Cross

<u>Page 206. Add after first sentence in first full paragraph on page:</u>

Do not be concerned that your planned cross will be relatively brief. "Cross-examination is . . . . more impression than . . . information." McElhaney, *Mongo on the Loose: Following Primitive Instincts Can Lead to Traps in the Courtroom*, 81 A.B.A.J. 80, 82 (July 1995).

§ 10.2(J) Conduct the Cross and Re-Cross

<u>Page 216. Add after "14 LITIGATION 25, 26-27 (Fall 1987)":</u>

Mr. Haynes believes that the first time you should purport to accept some responsibility for the problem. The next time the witness ventures beyond the scope of your question, begin subtly shifting blame to the witness: "Excuse me, I don't think you understood my question." Pozner & Dodd, *Controlling the Runaway Witness: Tried and True Techniques for Cross-Examination*, 27 TRIAL 110, 112 (Jan. 1991).

<u>Page 217. Add after the carryover paragraph on the top of the page:</u>

Sometimes, the witness's nonresponsiveness takes the form of undue delays before answering your question. In this situation, the natural temptation can be to press the witness for an immediate answer. In most cases, though, you should resist the temptation. Suppose that on direct examination, the witness answered confidently without delay. On cross-examination, the witness's demeanor becomes more tentative and takes a much longer time before beginning to answer the questions. The witness is playing into your hands. During summation, you will be able to contrast the witness's behavior on direct with his or her conduct on cross. Do not rush the witness. Give the witness enough rope--and time--to hang himself or herself.

§ 11.5 THE EXPERT'S MAJOR PREMISE

§ 11.5(A) The Law

Page 231. Add new paragraph at end of subsection:

Although the Supreme Court has abandoned Frye and shifted to the new empirical validation standard, the states remain free to decide which test they will employ to determine the admissibility of purportedly scientific testimony. According to one survey, 22 states remain committed to the Frye standard. Meaney, *From* Frye *to* Daubert: *Is a Pattern Unfolding*?, 35 JURIMETRICS 191, 193 (1995).

§ 11.6 THE EXPERT'S MINOR PREMISE

§ 11.6(A) The Law

Page 233. Add after the last paragraph in section:

In some jurisdictions, the courts equate the term "reasonably" in Rule 703 with "customarily." In those jurisdictions, under Rule 104(a), the judge decides whether such a custom exists in the specialty; and if the judge finds as a matter of fact that there is such a custom, the judge must allow the expert to rely on that type of information. The support for this view is dwindling. *In re Paoli R.R. Yard PCB Litigation*, 35 F.3d 717, 748 (3d Cir. 1994), *cert. denied*, 115 S.Ct. 1253 (1995). The trend is toward the view that even when that is the customary practice among experts in that field, the judge has residual discretion to preclude reliance on that type of information if the judge believes that reliance on that kind of data is objectively unreasonable.

CHAPTER 12. THE CROSS-EXAMINATION OF EXPERT WITNESSES--DEMYSTIFYING THE OPPOSING EXPERTS

§ 12.1 INTRODUCTION

Page 248. Insert after the citation to 253 J.AM.MED.ASS'N 2382 (1985):

The revelations of the Inspector General's 1997 report on the F.B.I. Crime Laboratory have heated up the controversy. *Justice Department Investigation of FBI Laboratory: Executive Summary*, 61 CR.L. 2017 (Apr. 16, 1997); Johnston, *Report Criticizes Scientific Testing at F.B.I. Crime Lab: "Serious" Problems Cited*, N.Y. TIMES, Apr. 16, 1997, at A1.

§ 12.8 ATTACKING THE EXPERT'S MINOR PREMISE

Page 254. Insert after third sentence in second full paragraph:

The opponent may file an *in limine* motion to challenge the reasonableness of the expert's reliance on the type of information underpinning the expert's opinion. *Thunder Hawk v. Union Pac. R.R.*, 891 P.2d 773 (Wyo. 1995). The trial judge might be more than willing to entertain the motion; if the proponent needs the expert's opinion to sustain his or her initial burden of production, the ruling on the *in limine* motion might obviate the necessity for a trial.

§ 14.2 THE GENERAL STRUCTURE OF A CLOSING ARGUMENT

§ 14.2(E) The Summation and Argument

Page 283. Add after the citation to KLONOFF & COLBY:

Do not be defensive about the fact that your witness occasionally said that he or she was uncertain or simply did not know about a particular matter. Instead, turn the witness's testimony to your advantage; argue that the witness's response is the best evidence of the witness's honesty. When the witness was uncertain, she said so; or when the witness did not know, he frankly conceded his ignorance.

Page 285. Add at the end of the carryover paragraph on the top of the page:

Tell the jury that "they caught a glimpse of the real M. Clayton Ransom on cross-examination." McElhaney, *Prepping the CEO*, 82 A.B.A.J. 84 (Oct. 1996).

Page 290. Add at the end of footnote 8:

In McCormick, *The Permissibility of Consequentialist Closing Arguments*, 38 TRIAL LAWYER'S GUIDE 399 (1994), the author argues that the propriety of a consequentialist argument depends on the type of case. When the jury must resolve a credibility or historical inference dispute, the jury has no business "consider[ing] the consequences of its decision." *Id.* at 405-07. In contrast, when the case is a legal standard dispute, the jurors must make a "normative judgment." *Id.* at 407-08. In this latter situation, the author contends that the courts ought to generally permit consequentialist arguments.

The debate over the propriety of "send a message" arguments is ongoing. Some jurisdictions allow such arguments in criminal cases but forbid them in civil actions. In *Carr v. State*, 480 S.E.2d 583 (Ga. 1997), the court approved a prosecutor's exhortation the jurors "send a message" to defendant and other criminals by convicting the defendant. However, a similar argument was held to be error in *F.D.I.C. v. Stahl*, 854 F.Supp. 1565 (S.D.Fla. 1994). That case involved an allegation of breach of fiduciary duty by officers and directors of a savings and loan. The plaintiff's attorney had argued that a verdict in the plaintiff's favor would "send the right message to directors around the country, they have got to be accountable." The court ruled that the argument was "inappropriate."

CHAPTER 15. TRIAL MOTIONS

§ 15.2 MOTION FOR A DIRECTED VERDICT

§ 15.2(A) Substance

Page 310. Add after the first complete sentence on the page:

E.g., *United States v. Quigley*, 53 F.3d 909 (8th Cir. 1995)(in a federal robbery prosecution, the government neglected to show the technical interstate commerce element).

§ 15.4 NEW TRIAL MOTIONS

§ 15.4(B) Procedure

Page 316. Add after second sentence in the section:

Criminal motions follows a similar pattern. Federal Rule of Criminal Procedure provides that after a guilty verdict, a new trial motion ordinarily "shall be made within 7 days after verdict." As *Carlisle v. United States*, 116 S.Ct. 1460 (1996) illustrates, the courts tend to strictly enforce the filing deadline.